Teddy
Bears

household history

Teddy Bears

Arlene Erlbach

Carolrhoda Books, Inc./Minneapolis

The photographs in this book are reproduced through the courtesy of: Bearb Ruth® © 1986 North American Bear Company, Inc. All rights reserved, cover (upper right), p. 34 (bottom); Corbis-Bettmann, cover (middle right), pp. 12, 14 (bottom), 15, 16 (bottom), 20 (both), 22, 28 (top), 29 (bottom); Jim Simondet/IPS, cover (lower right and upper left), pp. 2, 3, 21, 32 (bottom), 35, 38 (top), 43 (bottom); Archive Photos/Popperfoto, cover (lower left); Photri, pp. 1, 5, 11, 32 (top), 34 (top), 38 (bottom), 43 (top), 46; © Lani Novak Howe/Photri, pp. 6, 45 (upper right); © Christie's South Kensington, p. 7 (top); Margarete Steiff GmbH, pp. 7 (bottom), 25, 26; Good Bears of the World, pp. 8, 9; John Erste, pp. 10, 44–45; Archive Photos, pp. 13 (left), 17 (top), 41; UPI/Corbis-Bettmann, pp. 13 (right), 40 (top); Kunsthistorisches Museum, Vienna, p. 14 (top); San Diego Museum of Man, © Mrs. Julia E. Tuell, ca. 1900, p. 16 (top); IPS, pp. 17 (bottom), 37 (bottom); Louis Chester Walbridge Collection, Kansas Collection, University of Kansas Libraries, RH PH 21.240, p. 18 (bottom); Library of Congress, p. 18 (top); Museum of the City of New York, p. 19; Theodore Roosevelt Collection, Harvard College Library, pp. 23, 29 (top); National Museum of American History, Smithsonian Institution, neg. #74-797, p. 24; Brown Brothers, pp. 27, 28 (bottom), 30 (both), 31 (both), 39; Imperial War Museum, London, p. 33; Queen Elizabear® © 1982 North American Bear Company, Inc. All rights reserved, p. 35; The Teddy Bear Museum of Naples, p. 36; National Museum of American Art, Washington, D.C./Art Resource, NY, p. 37 (top); From the collection of the Central Children's Room, Donnell Library Center, The New York Public Library, p. 40 (bottom); National Archives, p. 42.

To Charlotte and Michael Herman, beary good friends.

The author wishes to acknowledge the assistance of the North American Bear Company, *Teddy Bear and Friend* magazine, the Toy Manufacturers of America, the Vermont Teddy Bear Company, and Mr. Ken Yenke, Good Bears of the World.

Words that appear in **bold** in the text are listed in the glossary on page 46.

This book is available in two editions:
Library binding by Carolrhoda Books, Inc.
Soft cover by First Avenue Editions
c/o The Lerner Publishing Group
241 First Avenue North, Minneapolis, MN 55401 U.S.A.

Library of Congress Cataloging-in-Publication Data

Erlbach, Arlene.
Teddy bears / by Arlene Erlbach.
   p.   cm. — (Household history)
   Includes index.
   Summary: Describes the history and popularity of teddy bears.
   ISBN: 1-57505-019-6 (lib. bdg.) ISBN: 1-57505-222-9 (pbk.)
   1. Teddy bears—Juvenile literature. [1. Teddy bears.] I. Title. II. Series.
NK8740.E75 1997
745.594'43—dc21   96-45021

Manufactured in the United States of America
1 2 3 4 5 6 – JR – 02 01 00 99 98 97

Contents

Nearly every American child has owned a teddy bear.

Hooray for the Teddy Bear!

You can tell your secrets to them and be sure that they won't be repeated. You can hug them as tight as you want. They're cuddly companions to take to bed. Hooray for the teddy bear, one of the most popular toys ever invented.

Almost every American owns a teddy bear before he or she reaches kindergarten. Every year, about forty million teddy bears are sold in the United States alone. That's enough to give a bear to almost every child between the ages of one and twelve.

Teddy bear collectors are known as **arctophiles** (ARK-toe-files), from the Greek words *arctos* (bear) and *philos* (love). One arctophile paid £110,000 (about $185,000), for the bear at left known as Teddy Girl.

Children aren't the only people who like teddy bears. Many adults love teddy bears and collect them. Adult collectors will pay hundreds or thousands of dollars for a rare or old bear. Every week, throughout the world, there are teddy bear shows, auctions, conventions, and fairs where people buy, sell, and trade bears.

In 1989, a couple paid $86,000 at an auction for a 63-year-old teddy bear. Paul and Rosemary Volpp of California, the people who bought the bear, already owned five thousand teddy bears. But they still wanted one more. They bought the bear to celebrate their wedding anniversary and named it Happy Anniversary.

Paul and Rosemary Volpp with Happy Anniversary.

Firefighters across the country rely on teddy bears to help comfort young fire victims.

Working Bears

Teddy bears are more than something to play with and collect. They're toys with personality. Teddy bears seem trustworthy, friendly, and almost human. To take advantage of these qualities, some teddy bears have been put to work. These bears help people in situations that make them feel uncomfortable.

Many doctors and dentists use teddy bears to comfort people when they are scared. Some hospitals have "bear clinics." Children take their bears to the clinic to learn about what happens in a hospital. If the children need to go to the hospital themselves, they'll know what to expect on their visit. If you stay in a hospital, your doctor may give you a bear to keep you company while you get well.

Many fire and police departments give bears to children who have been hurt by fire, crime, or abuse. Social workers, psychologists, and psychiatrists use teddy bears to make patients feel more secure. One teddy bear, named Spinoza, is designed with a cassette recorder zipped inside his belly. Kids insert tapes dealing with school, family, and friendship problems into Spinoza's recorder. As the cassette recorder plays, kids

The Washington, D.C., police department has recruited teddy bears to help out in situations where children need a friend.

feel like Spinoza is talking to them and helping them with their problems.

More Than Just Plush and Stuffing

Teddy bears mean a lot to many people, although they are a simple item that toy manufacturers call a **plush** toy. Plush toys contain stuffing. Plush also refers to the furry fabric that covers teddy bears. Plush toys are not complicated to make. You can make plush toys, including teddy bears, at home with a pattern or kit from a craft store. Most teddy bears, however, are made at toy factories.

Teddy bears are considered plush toys.

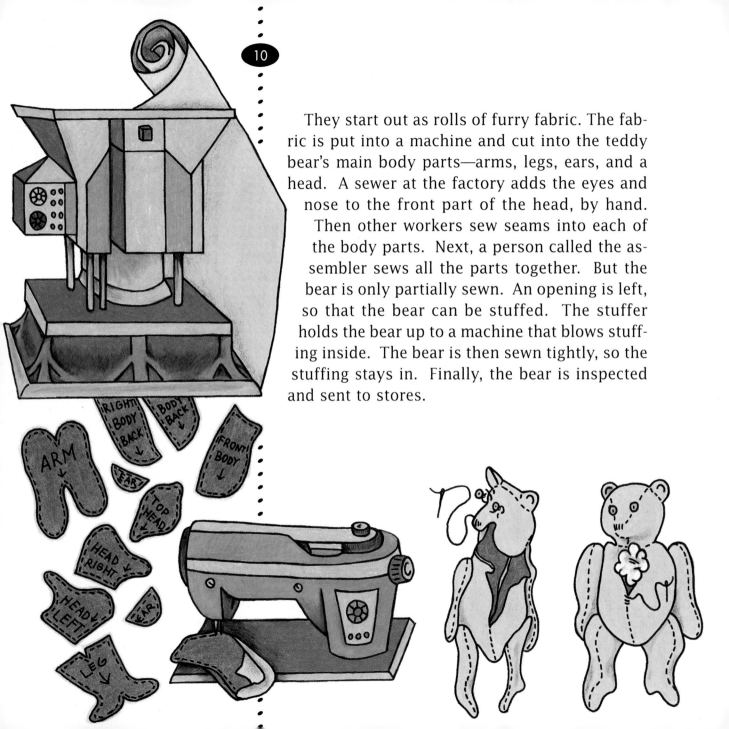

They start out as rolls of furry fabric. The fabric is put into a machine and cut into the teddy bear's main body parts—arms, legs, ears, and a head. A sewer at the factory adds the eyes and nose to the front part of the head, by hand. Then other workers sew seams into each of the body parts. Next, a person called the assembler sews all the parts together. But the bear is only partially sewn. An opening is left, so that the bear can be stuffed. The stuffer holds the bear up to a machine that blows stuffing inside. The bear is then sewn tightly, so the stuffing stays in. Finally, the bear is inspected and sent to stores.

This older teddy bear was passed down from one generation of bear lovers to another.

Teddy bears have been around for about one hundred years. So your parents, grandparents, and great-grandparents probably owned a bear. They may have even saved their teddy bears to remind them of the fun they had during childhood. Maybe they handed their bear down to you.

Why are so many people eager to have and to give bears? Why have bears been popular for so long? To discover how the teddy bear phenomenon happened, you'll need to go back a long time before teddy bears were invented. By taking a look at the history of toys, you'll find out how and when children first started to cuddle stuffed bears.

Even though teddy bears are fairly easy to make, there is something very special about them. That something special makes teddy bears the most popular plush toy of all. Over five hundred million dollars are spent on plush toys each year. Half of that money is from teddy bear buyers! Next on the stuffed animal popularity list come rabbits, dogs, and cats.

An ancient Egyptian wooden doll

How Bears Came to Be

As long as children have been around, adults have given them toys. In ancient times, children played with simple toys such as rattles made from dried gourds and primitive-looking dolls. They tossed round rocks or balls made from clay. Their toys weren't as elaborate as yours. Nor did they have many of them.

Only in the last one hundred and fifty years have children owned numerous toys and had time to play with them. Until then, children spent most of their time doing chores to help their families. Some children worked at jobs outside their homes. Nonetheless, adults have always needed something to amuse children, quiet them, or keep them out of mischief.

Although balls, rattles, and dolls are among some of the first known toys, they still remain popular. Toy animals have always delighted children, too. They appeal to both boys and girls. Sometimes a toy animal can take the place of a pet—without the work.

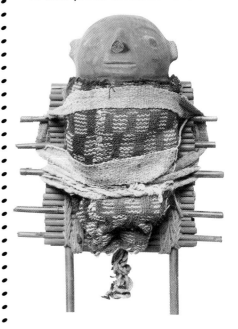

A doll from ancient Peru

Toys and games based on animals and animal shapes have been around for thousands of years. This Egyptian game is an ancestor of chess.

Right: The Flemish artist Pieter Brueghel the Elder painted this busy scene of children playing in 1560. A child rides on a hobby-horse in the center-left foreground.

Below: An early example of a hobbyhorse

Before Bears

Thousands of years ago, long before teddy bears, children played with toy animals such as clay horses, elephants, and goats. Egyptian children pushed and pulled wooden animals mounted on wheels. Greek children ran back and forth on **hobbyhorses,** toy horse heads mounted on poles.

During the Middle Ages, European children eagerly awaited the fair season from late summer to early autumn. This was the time of year when their parents could purchase toys for them, or at least children could see toys displayed. Traveling merchants set up booths in the center of town. These merchants sold a variety of toys, including carved wooden animals mounted on wire bases and hobbyhorses with bells attached.

By the mid-1600s, Germany had become the world center of toy making. German toys were sold all over Europe. Some of these toys came to North America when the first European settlers and their children arrived. The colonists' children had few toys and little time to play. Parents needed children to help work the land. When children had spare time, they most often spent it learning to read the Bible.

As America prospered, children had more time to play. By the 1700s, most cities in the American Colonies had at least one toy shop, and the bulk of the shop's merchandise was imported from Europe. Some children's toys came from these stores. But most toys were made at home by parents, grandparents, or older brothers and sisters.

Brought to the American Colonies by Dutch settlers, this rocking horse was made by hand in the 1600s.

Right: Native American girls play with homemade toys.

Below: St. Nicholas, or Santa Claus, pauses between stops delivering toys.

Native American children also generally played with homemade toys. The youngest Native Americans played with turtle-shell or deer-hoof rattles. Leather balls, dolls made from corn husks or animal hides, and toy animals carved from wood and bone were also popular.

By the early 1800s, toys had become quite common throughout the United States. So had the idea of Christmas as a time for giving gifts among Christian Americans. The poem *A Visit from St. Nicholas,* which you may know as *The Night before Christmas,* helped make the Christmas gift-giving custom popular. Christmas became an enormous factor in the toy business.

The toy industry grew in the United States during the 1800s. American children no longer had to wait for the latest toy to be shipped from Europe. By the end of the century, hundreds of companies began to manufacture toys in North America. An entire industry devoted to children developed. Dolls, balls, and toy animals still remained popular, but there were new favorites.

One of the most popular animal toys was Noah's ark. It consisted of a wooden model of the ark, Noah's family, and numerous pairs of animals. In many homes, because of its biblical connection, the ark was the only toy that children could play with on Sunday. Elaborate arks contained hundreds of carved wooden animals. Children spent hours arranging them in pairs.

Above: By the 1800s, American shops stocked toys made in Europe and in the United States.

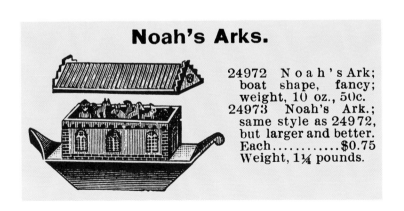

Noah's Arks.

24972 Noah's Ark; boat shape, fancy; weight, 10 oz., 50c.
24973 Noah's Ark; same style as 24972, but larger and better. Each...........$0.75 Weight, 1¼ pounds.

Left: A mail order catalog from the late 1800s advertises the popular Noah's ark toy.

Children in the late 1800s could choose from a variety of toys made from tin and wood. However, few soft, cuddly toys were available.

Toy makers made tin animals, too, particularly horses. The horse, with or without its attached carriage, was the transportation of the day. Children played with tin horses just as you might play with toy cars.

Searching for a Softer Toy

Although children played with wooden and tin animals, soft stuffed animals were not common. Those few soft stuffed toys found in American homes were usually rag dolls, not animals. Mothers generally made these dolls at home from clothing scraps. They weren't something you'd normally buy at a toy store. The soft toys available in shops were made by local craftspeople and didn't look much different from those made at home.

In the 1870s, however, people's ideas about stuffed toys changed. Women's magazines began to publish sew-it-yourself patterns for stuffed animals, along with knitting and embroidery patterns. These animals took some time and skill to construct. The person making the animal needed to cut out the paper pattern pieces and pin them onto cloth. Then they had to carefully cut the cloth and sew the animal's parts together. Only someone with a good deal of leisure would have the time to do all this.

Soon however, Arnold Print Works, a company in Massachusetts, turned stuffed toy construction into a simple task. The company printed realistic animal pictures on yards of fabric. These pictures could be easily cut, stuffed, and sewn. The picture was printed in two parts, back and front. There were no complicated patterns or separate body parts to attach. Many children in the late 1800s perfected their sewing skills while putting these toy animals together.

A pattern for Tatters the dog, from Arnold Print Works

Arnold Print Works's animal patterns were very popular. The company sold many designs, including a dog, a cat, a rabbit, a rooster, and an owl. Arnold Print Works didn't produce a bear, but this doesn't mean that people hadn't been thinking about that animal and its appeal.

Bear Appeal

Bears have fascinated people for hundreds of years. By the late 1800s, bears were popular attractions in many American circuses and zoos.

Trained bears were once a common sight in cities and towns.

Bears appear to be almost human. They can stand on two feet, just as people do. Although bears are wild animals and can be vicious, they look almost as friendly as dogs, particularly when they are young. These characteristics have always intrigued humans.

In other parts of the world and in other cultures, children already played with toy bears. Russian children had ceramic or wooden bears called Mishkas, based on a Russian folklore character. English children enjoyed a mechanical bear, which they called a bruin. Some Native American parents gave their children bear-shaped kachina dolls for good luck.

Although most American children didn't play with toy bears, they saw bears in a variety of places—not just in zoos. More and more during the 1800s, American advertisers took advantage of the animal's humanlike appearance. The Pettijohn Company used bears in their ads for a breakfast cereal. This may have had a connection to the story of Goldilocks, the Three Bears, and their porridge. The Behr Piano Company featured bears in their ads, too.

By the early 1900s, Americans were used to seeing bears promote products. They were also used

Realistic stuffed animal toys on wheels—including bears—were popular in the early 1900s, but they weren't the kind of toy you'd want to hug.

to having stuffed toys around the house. Then a minor political event brought the teddy bear to market and changed the toy business forever.

The Teddy Bear's Big Break

In November 1902, United States President Theodore Roosevelt visited Mississippi and Louisiana to settle a land dispute. Neither state could decide where its boundary should be.

While on this trip, the president entertained himself by bear hunting. Hunting was Roosevelt's favorite sport, but on this trip he wasn't having much luck. One of the men in his party cornered a bear. He tied it up for the president to shoot. Roosevelt refused. He felt it was unfair to kill a cornered bear.

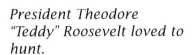

President Theodore "Teddy" Roosevelt loved to hunt.

DRAWING
THE LINE
IN MISSISSIPPI

In his cartoon for the Washington Post, *Clifford Berryman made much of the president's refusal to shoot a bear. The actual bear was quite large, but Berryman added to the drama by drawing a small, frightened cub.*

Political cartoonist Clifford Berryman drew a cartoon about the incident. It was published in the *Washington Post* and reprinted in other newspapers. The simple cartoon was titled "Drawing the Line in Mississippi." The title referred to the boundary between the disputing states and to the president's gesture toward the cornered bear.

This early example of one of "Teddy's Bears," made by the Michtoms, is now at the Smithsonian Institution in Washington, D.C.

Rose and Morris Michtom, a Brooklyn, New York, couple, saw the cartoon, and it gave them an idea. Rose Michtom made two jointed, plush-covered bears by hand. She stuffed the bears with straw and used buttons for their eyes. Then she displayed them in the window of the couple's candy and stationery shop. Being Russian immigrants, the Michtoms may have been aware of a toy bear's child appeal. Whether Rose was thinking of Russian Mishkas or not, her bears did have loads of appeal. They sold out the same day, and the Michtoms received orders for more.

Morris Michtom wrote to President Roosevelt, asking if he and Rose could call their creations "Teddy's Bears." The president approved the idea, not realizing the stir that the toy would soon create. Within a few years, teddy bears had become so popular that the Michtoms were in the toy business full-time. They eventually changed the toy's name to teddy bear and formed the Ideal Novelty and Toy Company.

The Big Bear Origin Debate

The Michtoms designed the first teddy bear, but not everyone agrees that they invented the first soft stuffed bear. Margarete Steiff of Germany may have invented one around the time the Michtoms did—or even a little before the Michtoms produced their bear.

As a child, Margarete Steiff contracted polio. The disease paralyzed her legs, so she used a wheelchair. It also weakened her right arm, but Margarete learned to sew. By the time she was thirty, she owned her own clothing store. Later, she formed Steiff toys, a company that produced soft stuffed animals. (Founded in the late 1800s, the company is still in business and is one of the world's largest producers of stuffed animals.)

Margarete Steiff (at left) created countless stuffed animals. (Her last name, Steiff, rhymes with life.)

*Richard Steiff,
Margarete's nephew*

In 1897 Margarete's nephew Richard, an artist, went to the Stuttgart Zoo. He drew a sketch of a bear family he saw there and then showed it to his aunt. Richard's sketch was so appealing that Margarete decided to make a stuffed toy bear. In 1903 Richard displayed the bear at a trade show in Leipzig, Germany. Few people noticed it. Finally, toward the end of the fair, an American toy buyer did. He ordered three thousand bears. Soon the original order had been sold and more Steiff bears were on their way to America.

Margarete Steiff deserves credit for being the first person to mass-produce soft stuffed animals. But she would have had no reason to call her stuffed bear a teddy bear. She had probably never seen the cartoon of Teddy Roosevelt and the cornered bear; it wasn't the type of story that was of international interest.

The Bear Invasion Begins

Whoever first created the bear, his or her timing couldn't have been better. Teddy bears hit the United States market at a time when more Americans lived in towns and cities. Without farm chores to keep them busy, children had more time to play.

In the early 1900s, teddy bears began appearing all over America—even on city streets.

Between the 1860s and the early 1900s, the toy business expanded rapidly. More than three hundred factories opened in the United States. By 1906 many of these factories were making teddy bears. Factories opened in every major American city to satisfy public demand.

What made these toys so popular? Along with good timing, the teddy bear had one more thing going for it—broad appeal.

Originally, toy makers thought teddy bears would appeal only to boys.

Right: A fashionable young woman warms up to a teddy bear muff.

Crazy for Bears

At first, toy manufacturers and stores thought the teddy bear would be a boy's toy. If boys didn't want to be seen playing with dolls, toy makers reasoned they might play with a bear instead. Girls changed that idea fast. They wanted teddy bears, too.

Children weren't the only ones who wanted bears. In the early 1900s, fashionable young ladies carried their teddy bears to restaurants and to the beach. Wealthy young men took bears for rides on bicycles and in the new invention the horseless carriage, better known as the car.

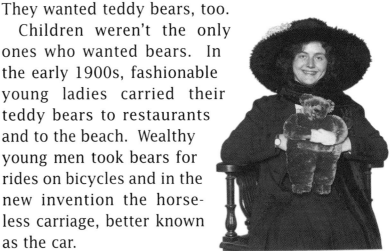

Teddy Roosevelt became so identified with the teddy bear that English students at Cambridge (left) used one to greet the former president when he visited in 1910. Roosevelt's famous hunting trip also inspired toy manufacturers to create metal banks (below) and other toys.

New immigrants liked teddy bears, too. The bear came to symbolize the United States and one of America's most popular presidents, Teddy Roosevelt. When the president made appearances, teddy bears and American flags often decorated the stage. To new immigrants, having a teddy bear was part of becoming an American. The toy represented opportunity—both to play and to be free.

Girls quickly decided that they wanted teddy bears, too.

More Than Just a Fad

The teddy bear's popularity worried doll makers at first. But despite the teddy bear craze, dolls still sold well. Some people thought that teddy bears were a fad and would shortly go out of style. A few people thought bears were a menace to motherhood, since many girls preferred teddy bears to dolls. These people worried that if girls played with teddy bears instead of dolls, they might not be prepared, later in life, to be mothers. Despite these fears, the teddy bear craze continued.

Early teddy bears looked more realistic than modern bears. They had a hump on their backs, longer limbs, **mohair** coverings, and a more triangular head. They even sounded more like real bears, because many contained a device called a **growler** that made a growling sound. Their stuffing was different, too. Early bears contained straw, wood shavings, or **kapok,** a silky fiber that comes from a tropical seedpod.

Manufacturers created other stuffed animals such as monkeys, rabbits, and dogs to compete with teddy bears. These toys sold well, but certainly not like bears. A few manufacturers produced another politically inspired stuffed toy called Billy Possum, in honor of President William Taft. Taft served immediately after Teddy Roosevelt. His favorite meal was potatoes and opossum. Billy Possum never reached the teddy bear's popularity, but the toy sold for the years of William Taft's term as president.

Left: An early teddy bear

Wood shavings were used to stuff many early bears.

Koala bear toys are especially popular in Australia.

Bears the World Over

As bears became popular in America, their popularity also grew in other parts of the world. While American teddy bears had triangular faces, British bears had rounder faces and shorter noses and limbs. The French produced thinner bears. An early Japanese bear had large pointed ears and enormous paws.

Australian children have cuddled many versions of the teddy bear, including one covered in sheepskin. They have their own national bear toy, too, the koala bear. Koalas are not actually bears. They're **marsupials,** in the same family as the short-lived Billy Possum. But koala bears are just as popular with Australian kids as teddy bears are in the United States.

As long as there have been teddy bears, manufacturers have taken advantage of technology to produce unusual and novel bears. A 1907 bear's eyes lit up when you squeezed its chest. Another did the same thing when you lifted its right paw.

In the 1960s, mechanical, battery-operated bears became popular. These bears imitated all kinds of human activity, from playing musical instruments to vacuuming the floor.

Bear toys have been designed to do all kinds of things, including cleaning eyeglasses!

Bear Safety

In 1969 the United States government passed laws to ensure that toys, including teddy bears, would be safe for children. Four years later, the United States Safety Commission was formed. Because of the commission's laws, your bear's eyes must be plastic so they won't break and must be attached with bolts so they can't be swallowed. Stuffings are more fire resistant than in the past. The bear's seams must be strong so that they cannot break open. All these precautions make your teddy bear safer to play with.

During World War II, girls worked in Britain's teddy bear factories, stuffing bears by hand. In modern factories, inspectors make sure every new bear is safely and properly made.

A gathering of bears—or bear lovers—is sometimes called a den.

This well-dressed character bear was inspired by professional baseball players.

Bears with Character

Teddy bear lovers often think their bears have personalities attached to them. Many toy manufacturers take advantage of this teddy bear feature. Bear artists, people who make teddy bears for collectors, also put a lot of personality in their bears. Both toy makers and bear artists design many types of character bears.

A homemade bear with a lot of personality inspired an entire toy company. In 1979 a New York woman named Barbara Isenberg made a teddy bear out of sweatshirt material for her son.

This group of collectible bears includes, from the left, Peef, Snuggle, Queen Elizabear, and an unnamed bear handcrafted by a bear artist.

She called it Albert the Running Bear. Albert was such a hit that Barbara formed the North American Bear Company. The company produces bears for special occasions, such as Bat Mitz Bear, and bears based on famous people, such as Amelia Bearhart, Abearham Lincoln, and Queen Elizabear.

Teddy bears have come a long way from the first stuffed toys sewn by Rose Michtom and Margarete Steiff. But if modern bears don't look exactly like the earliest teddy bears, children still hug them, cuddle them, and take them to bed.

Over the years, the teddy bear's purpose hasn't changed much. It has only been expanded upon.

Beyond Bears

Bear statues romp outside the Teddy Bear Museum of Naples, Florida.

The toy that some people thought was just a fad—or menace to motherhood—is here to stay. It's hard to imagine a life without teddy bears. They've become a symbol of childhood, but they're not only children's toys. Adults buy older antique bears and new bears, designed for collectors by teddy bear artists. Bear collecting is so popular that half a dozen magazines are published for bear enthusiasts.

Several museums in the world specialize in teddy bears. The Teddy Bear Museum of Naples, Florida, houses more than three thousand teddy bears. Outside the museum, bronze and marble teddy bear sculptures welcome visitors. You can also see bears displayed at London's Museum of Childhood, the Margaret Woodbury Strong Museum in Rochester, New York, and the Steiff Museum in Germany.

Even fine artists have been inspired by teddy bears. Artist Robert Brackman features a well-loved bear in his painting Somewhere in America.

Inspired by Bears

Ever since the teddy bear was invented, the toy has inspired toy makers, designers, and artists. Shortly after teddy bears became popular, manufacturers began producing merchandise such as postcards, silverware, board games, and muffs decorated with bears. One children's clothing company produced mohair coats that looked like teddy bear fur. In addition to playing with a teddy bear, a child could look like one!

A teddy bear coat from the early 1900s

Bears turn up on all kinds of products and in all kinds of places, from the bottom of a cereal bowl to the sides of tennis shoes to the pages of books.

This koala has a pouch for holding books.

Nowadays, you'll find bears on clothing, stationery, bandages, dishes, jewelry, and even diapers. You can eat teddy bears, too. Food manufacturers make teddy-bear-shaped cookies, candies, crackers, and pretzels.

Teddy bears have inspired many people to write—and sing—songs. Between 1907 and 1911, the early teddy bear years, over four hundred songs were written using the words *bear* or *teddy bear.* One of the most enduring bear songs, *The Teddy Bears' Picnic,* has become the theme song for many teddy bear gatherings.

At this teddy bear party in the early 1900s, prizes were awarded to the owners of the bears with the "kindliest expressions."

In 1979 thousands of people and their teddy bears showed up for the world's first real teddy bear picnic in England. The picnic was sponsored by Good Bears of the World, an organization that provides bears to people who need a soft, cuddly friend.

Along with taking their bears to picnics, many bear enthusiasts celebrate Good Bear Day on October 27, President Roosevelt's birthday. On Good Bear Day, bear lovers hold picnics, attend events involving teddy bears, and raise money for Good Bears of the World.

Be a good bear. Promote good cheer through Good Bears of the World. For information, write:

Good Bears of the World
Box 13097
Toledo, OH 43613

In real life, Christopher Robin Milne wasn't always happy to be associated with Winnie-the-Pooh.

The original teddy bear (on which Winnie-the-Pooh was based) is joined by other residents of the Hundred Acre Wood.

Bears in Print and Beyond

You don't have to go to a picnic to celebrate teddy bears. Bears can be found between the pages of books, on the television screen, and beyond. One child's love for his own bear turned into the classic book and cartoon series, Winnie-the-Pooh. Written by A. A. Milne, the boy's father, the stories follow the adventures of Christopher Robin and his teddy bear, fondly known as Pooh.

A statue at the London Zoo honors Winnie-the-Pooh, who is probably one of the world's most famous teddy bears. At times, however, the real Christopher Robin Milne wished that Winnie-the-Pooh had never been created. Christopher Robin's schoolmates teased him because of his association with the famous bear.

A statue at London's Paddington Station honors another famous bear—Paddington. When he arrived by train at the station for which he was named, Paddington wore a tag which read, "Please Look After This Bear, Thank You." A British family adopted the bear, and Paddington's adventures with them have since been the subject of many books written by Michael Bond. Oddly enough, Paddington Bear comes from Peru, where no bears live.

Corduroy, the bear missing a button on his overalls, has been featured in books written by Don Freeman. The Berenstain Bears, created by Stan and Jan Berenstain, have their own series of books, focusing on the problems of growing up. They've starred in videos and in their own cartoon show, too.

Teddy bears have inspired writers around the world. Australian children read about Blinky Bill, a mischievous koala. French children are familiar with a series of books by Claude Lebrun featuring the Little Brown Bear. English children follow the adventures of Rupert Bear, a comic strip character.

The Roosevelt Bears, two well-dressed and well-traveled bears, were the heroes of a series of stories written in the early 1900s.

Bears Who Take a Stand

Bears have been the spokes-animal for a variety of causes. In England, William Bear raises money for a cancer hospital. Another British bear raises money for mentally disturbed children. And Smokey Bear reminds the American public about preventing forest fires. The first Smokey Bear toy was produced in 1953 by Ideal Toys, founded by Rose and Morris Michtom.

Rose Michtom and Margarete Steiff couldn't have known what they were starting when they stitched together the very first plush teddy bears.

Smokey Bear has long been a spokes-animal for preventing forest fires.

Soft, stuffed, and appealing, the teddy bear marked a change in the history of toys and in the history of childhood.

From its beginnings in the early 1900s, the teddy bear has filled a need for durable and safe mass-produced toys. It has also become an enduring symbol of childhood that appeals to people of all ages in countries around the world. Hooray for the teddy bear, one of the world's most popular toys!

Sometimes meeting an old bear is like meeting an old friend.

More than just plush and stuffing, the teddy bear is one of the world's most popular toys.

Have a Teddy Bear Picnic!

Invite your friends and their bears to a teddy bear picnic at your house. Before your guests arrive, make plans.

You Will Need:

for the invitations

tracing paper

pencil

scissors

colored construction paper

colored markers

glue

1. To make your invitations, take a piece of tracing paper and place it over the outline at left. Trace around the bear shape with a pencil. Cut out the tracing paper shape with scissors.

Fold a sheet of colored construction paper in half. Place the tracing paper shape along the fold and draw around it with a pencil. Cut out the bear shape.

Decorate the outside using colored markers or gluing on bits of paper.

On the inside, write something like this:

You and your favorite teddy bear are invited to a teddy bear picnic.

Date: _____

Time: _____

Place: _____

Given by: *(your name and the name of your teddy bear)*

When you send the invitations, include your friend's name and the name of your friend's bear in the address.

2. At the picnic, serve potato chips, sandwiches, cookies, and punch or lemonade. Look for bear-shaped cookies or crackers at the grocery store. And don't forget to put some honey in your picnic basket for the bears!

3. Hold contests with prizes, letting everyone vote on who has the biggest bear, the smallest bear, the cutest bear, the oldest bear, or the best-dressed bear. Or get everyone together to sing *The Teddy Bears' Picnic.* Whatever you do, have a *beary* good time!

You Will Need:

for the picnic

sandwiches

potato chips

punch or lemonade

bear-shaped cookies and crackers

prizes for contest winners (gummi bears make good prizes)

Glossary

arctophiles: people who love bears

growler: a device inside a teddy bear that makes a growling sound when the bear's body is moved forward

hobbyhorses: toys that consist of a pole with a toy horse's head attached to one end. With a hobby-horse, a child can pretend that he or she is riding on horseback.

kapok: a silky fiber from the seeds of the ceiba tree. Kapok was once used to stuff mattresses, teddy bears, and sleeping bags.

marsupials: members of a group of mammals, including opossums and koalas, in which females generally have a pouch on the abdomen for carrying their young

mohair: yarn or cloth made from the fur of the Angora goat

plush: a soft toy containing stuffing. Also, the soft fabric used to cover the toy.

Books on Bears

The Adventures of Albert, the Running Bear. Written by Barbara Isenberg & Susan Wolf. Illustrated by Dick Gackenbach. Albert finds himself running in a marathon after growing fat from eating too many snacks.

A Bear Called Paddington. Written by Michael Bond and illustrated by Peggy Fortnum. Paddington, a bear from Peru, is adopted by the Brown family in England.

The Berenstain Bears' New Baby. Written and illustrated by Stan & Jan Berenstain. The Berenstain Bears prepare for a new addition in the family by building a new bed for Small Bear.

Corduroy. Written and illustrated by Don Freeman. Corduroy, a bear who lives in a department store, searches for a missing button on his overalls—and for a friend.

Dear Bear. Written and illustrated by Joanna Harrison. Katie, a young girl, befriends and writes letters to a bear who lives under the stairs in her house.

Don't You Dare Shoot That Bear. Written and illustrated by Robert Quackenbush. In this story about Theodore Roosevelt, readers learn how the teddy bear got its name.

Polar, the Titanic Bear. Written by Daisy Corning Stone Spedden and illustrated by Laurie McGaw. Polar, young Master's toy bear, travels with an American family on holiday overseas, witnessing the sinking of the *Titanic* and briefly becoming separated from his owner.

The Teddy Bear Habit. Written by James Collier. Set in the 1960s, this story follows the attempts of a twelve-year-old boy to kick his teddy bear "habit" and make it into a rock and roll band.

The Teddy Bears' Picnic. Written by Jimmy Kennedy and illustrated by Alexandra Day. Teddy bears from all over gather in the woods for a picnic and fun and games.

Winnie-the-Pooh. Written by A. A. Milne and illustrated by Ernest H. Shepard. Young Christopher Robin and his bear friend, Edward, nicknamed Winnie-the-Pooh, explore the Hundred Acre Wood.

Index